# In the Sea

## David Elliott
### illustrated by Holly Meade

CANDLEWICK PRESS

First paperback edition 2014

The Library of Congress has cataloged the hardcover edition as follows:
Elliott, David, date.
In the sea / David Elliott ; illustrated by Holly Meade. — 1st ed.
p.  cm.
ISBN 978-0-7636-4498-7 (hardcover)
ISBN 978-0-7636-7050-4 (paperback)
1.  Marine animals—Juvenile poetry. 2.  Children's poetry, American.
I. Meade, Holly, ill. II. Title.
PS3555.L567415  2012
811'.54—dc22  2010047666

APS 21 20 19
10 9 8 7 6

Printed in Humen, Dongguan, China

This book was typeset in Columbus Semi Bold.
The illustrations are woodblock prints and watercolor.

Candlewick Press
99 Dover Street
Somerville, Massachusetts 02144

visit us at www.candlewick.com

To the Gulf of Mexico and all that depends on it
D. E.

For my grandson, soon to be born.
Though I have yet to look into your face and cradle
you in my arms, I Love you Entirely.
H. M.

## The Sea Horse

See the sea horse in the sea.
Where else would the sea horse be?
For though it's dainty as a wish,
the sea horse is, you see, a fish.

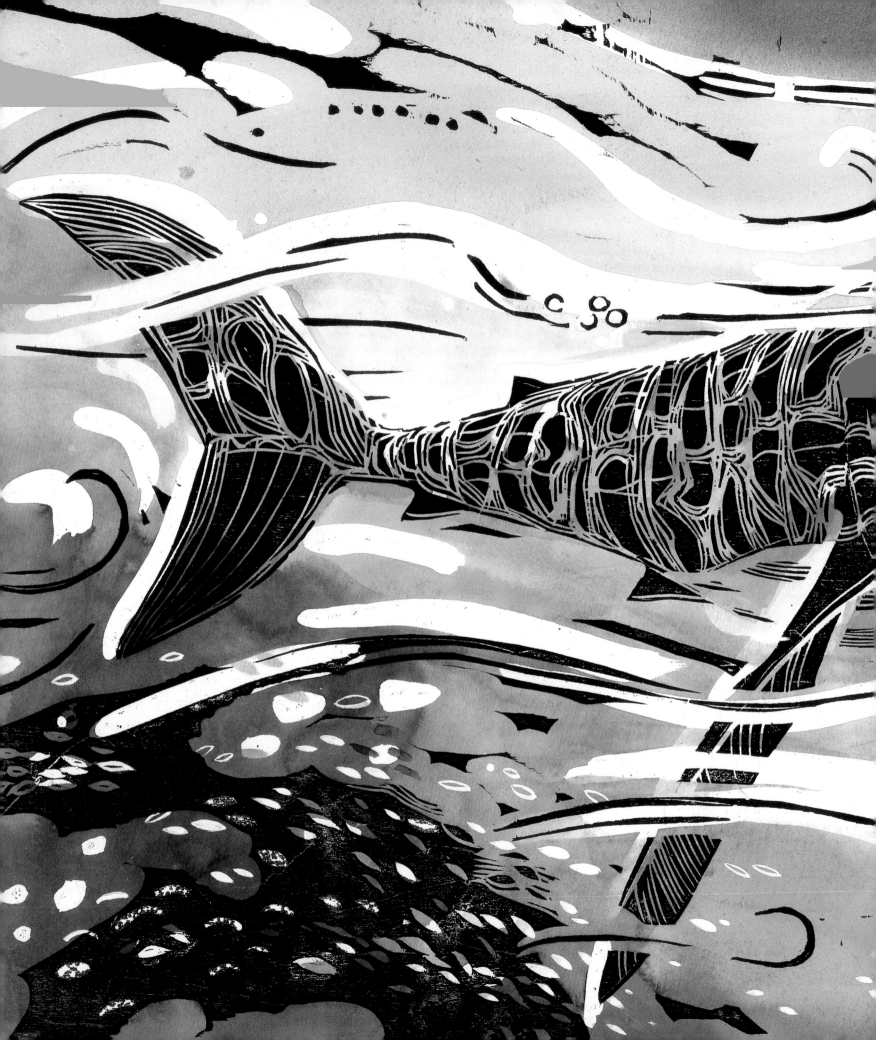

topus

ar out of the blue,
-armed apparition,
nish in a cloud of ink.
st, but a magician.

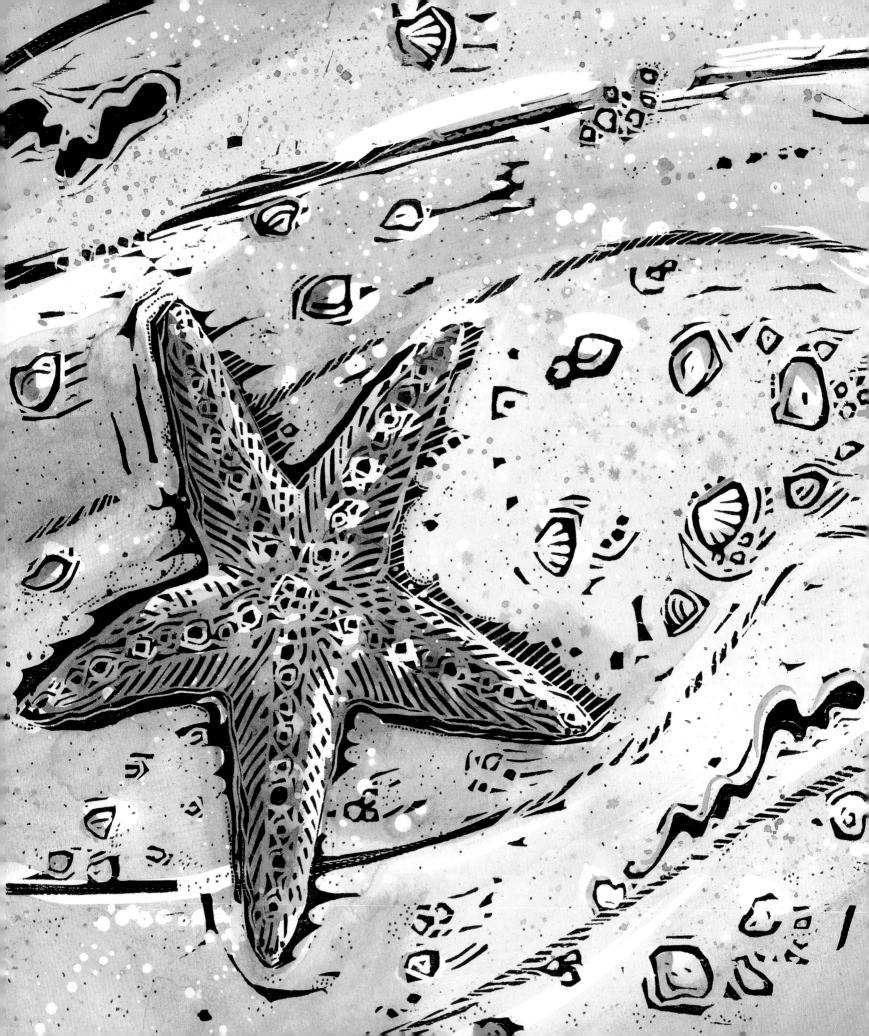

## The Starfish

Five fingers,
like a hand,
the starfish shines
in a sky of sand.

**The Urchin**

Spiny.

**The Sardine**

Tiny.

**The Mackerel**
Shiny.

**The Shrimp**
Briny.

# The Herring

Nobody's fool.
How could she be?
She lives in a school!

## The Dolphin

He jumps.
He leaps.
He twirls.
He spins.
He's the jester
of the briny deep,
an acrobat with fins.

## The Orca

You breach the water's surface
in your black-and-white tuxedo,
then disappear into the blue,
an elegant torpedo.

### The Sea Turtle

Swims the seven seas
for thirty years,
then finds the beach
where she was born—
by magic, it appears.

How can she know to come upon
that far and sandy place?
Rare instrument of nature,
fair compass in a carapace.

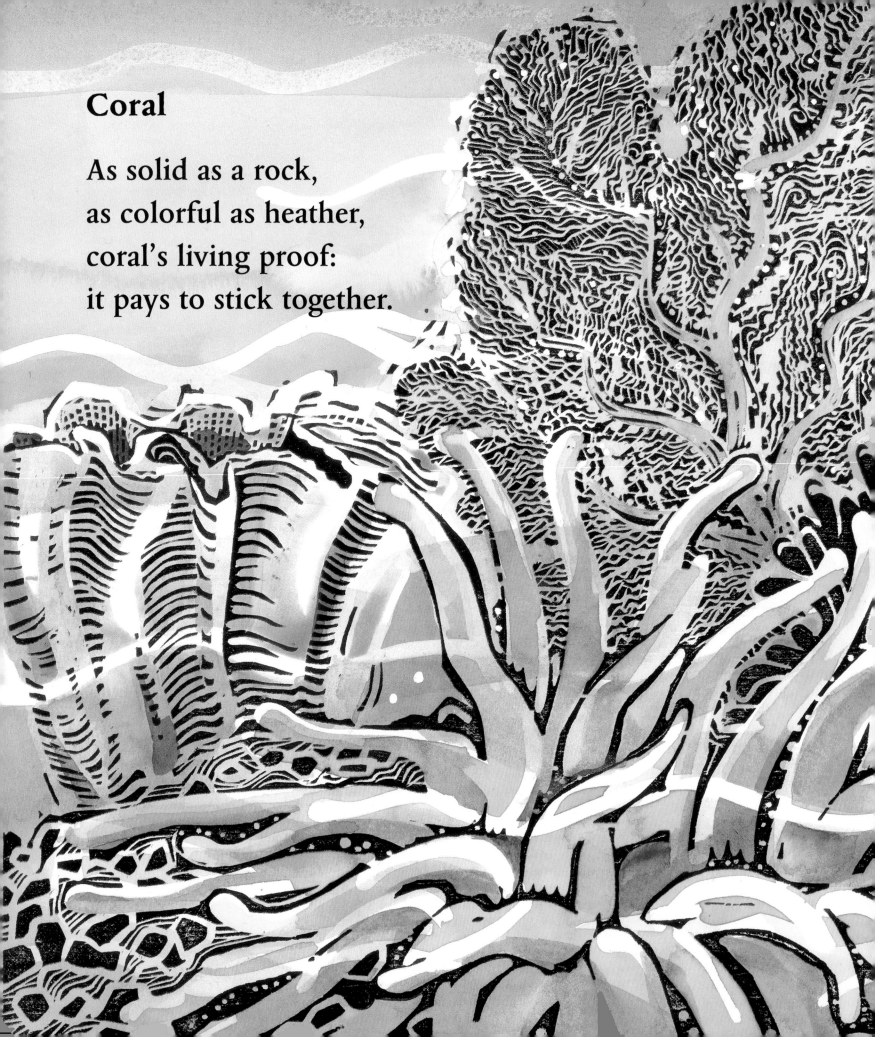

## Coral

As solid as a rock,
as colorful as heather,
coral's living proof:
it pays to stick together.

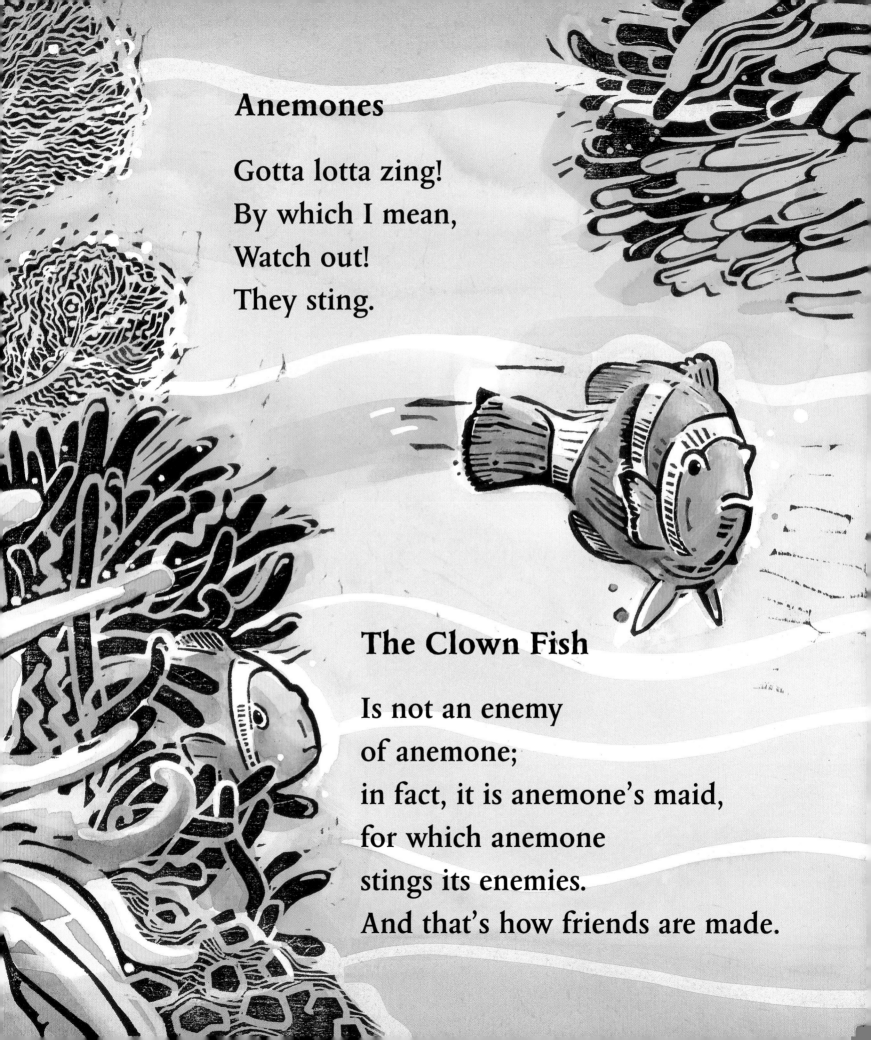

## Anemones

Gotta lotta zing!
By which I mean,
Watch out!
They sting.

## The Clown Fish

Is not an enemy
of anemone;
in fact, it is anemone's maid,
for which anemone
stings its enemies.
And that's how friends are made.

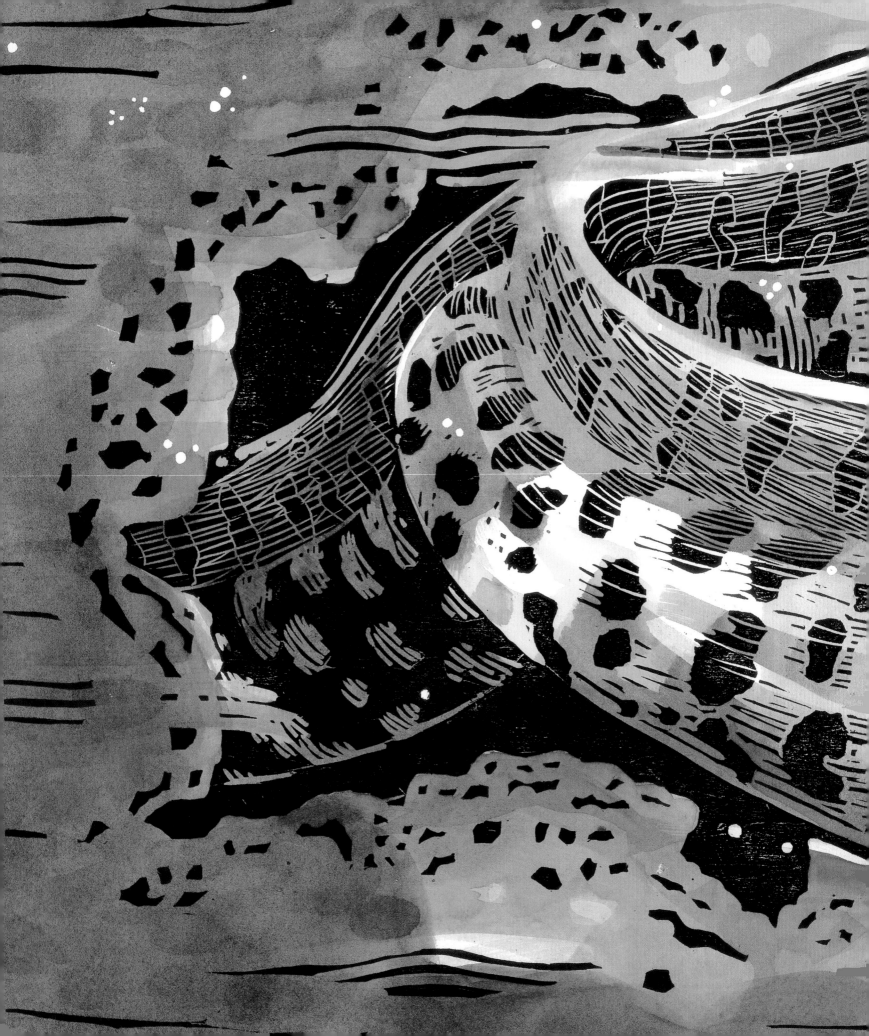

## The Moray Eel

Ferocious. Cunning.
Belligerent. Brave.
A sword without its sheath,
a dragon in its cave.

## The Chambered Nautilus

Her shell spins round,
a top
a dancer
a staircase with no end
a question with no answer.

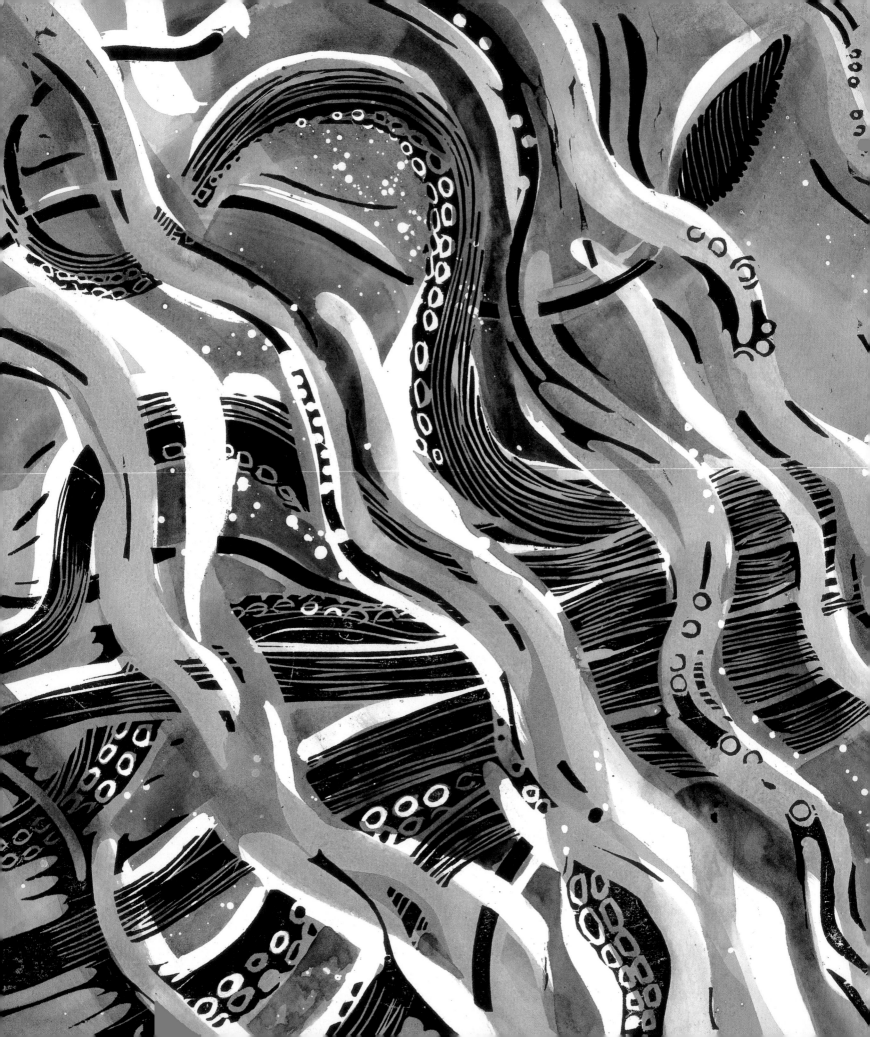

## The Giant Squid

Few have seen him.
Few wish to.
Hide from this one!
(That's what fish do.)

# The Puffer Fish

A trickster.
A clown.
A magician.
A buffoon.
One minute
she's a fish;
the next,
she's a balloon.

## The Blue Whale

Rises to the surface,
an island, a mountain.
All fluke and fin and fountain,

the largest animal alive

sings a chanty deep and slow
of winds that rage and storms that blow,
of shipwrecked sailors down below—
oh, where they are we cannot go—

and then . . .

she dives!